KU-512-130

Pocket Edition 100 FACTS

OCEANS

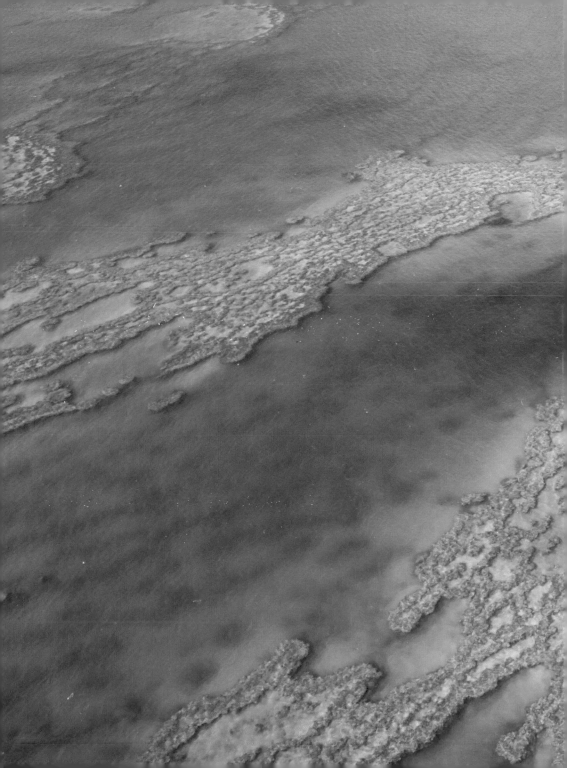

Pocket Edition

100 FACTS

OCEANS

Clare Oliver

Consultant: Clive Carpenter

Miles Kelly

First published in 2002 by Miles Kelly Publishing Ltd
Harding's Barn, Bardfield End Green, Thaxted, Essex, CM6 3PX, UK

Copyright © Miles Kelly Publishing 2002

This edition updated 2014, published 2019, printed 2021

4 6 8 10 9 7 5 3

Publishing Director Belinda Gallagher
Creative Director Jo Cowan
Editorial Director Rosie Neave
Assistant Editor Amy Johnson
Cover Designer Rob Hale
Designers Rob Hale, John Christopher (White Design), Venita Kidwai
Image Manager Liberty Newton
Production Controller Jennifer Brunwin
Reprographics Stephan Davis
Assets Lorraine King

All rights reserved. No part of this publication may be reproduced, stored in a retrieval
system, or transmitted by any means, electronic, mechanical, photocopying, recording
or otherwise, without the prior permission of the copyright holder.

ISBN 978-1-78617-767-4

Printed in China

British Library Cataloguing-in-Publication Data
A catalogue record for this book is available from the British Library

ACKNOWLEDGEMENTS

The publishers would like to thank the following sources for the use of their photographs:
Key: t = top, b = bottom, c = centre, l = left, r = right, m = main, bg = background

Cover (front) melissaf84/ Shutterstock, (back, cr) Stephen Rees/Shutterstock
Dreamstime 23(bl) Biolifepics; 30(m) Bluesunphoto; 42(c) Perstock; 43(cr) Bladerunner88; 45(cr) Expozer
FLPA 24(t) Tui De Roy/Minden Pictures; 27(c) Norbert Wu/Minden Pictures **Fotolia** 34(c) (paper) pdtnc
iStock 9(b) Joshua Haviv; 34(b) brytta **NPL** 25(r) Jurgen Freund; 26(t) David; Shale; 28(m) Doug Perrine
Rex 38–39 W. Disney/Everett **Shutterstock** 1 and 21(t) Luna Vandoorne; 2–3 and 14(tr) agrosse; 5(tl) Richard Peterson,
(tr) and 35(b) ANCH, (b) EpicStockMedia; 6–7(bg) Aubrey Laughlin, (m) ktsdesign; 11(t) fashcool, (b) Regien Paassen;
16–17(t) Boris Pamikov; 16(br) cynoclub; 17(b) Lynsey Allan; 19(b) Ian Scott; 20–21 powell'sPoint; 20(b) Eric Isselee; 22–23 Mariusz
Potocki; 22(l) worldswildlifewonders; 23(t) Vladimir Melnik; 24(b) David Evison; 28(b) Arto Hakola; 29(m) foryouinf, (t) AridOcean;
30(b) Andrea Ricordi; 31(t) Gail Johnson, (bl) Jenny Leonard, (br) Mariko Yuki; 32–33 Rich Lindie; 32(t) steve estvanik; 33(br) BMJ;
34(t) DJTaylor; 35(t) Mark Hall; 36–37(bg) ilolab; 39(tr) Andrew Jalbert; 41(t) JonMilnes; 43(b) Dave Turner, (b) Ruth Peterkin;
44(m) Jeanne Provost, (b) CLChang; 45(t) Gustavo Miguel Fernandes, (b) Darren Brode

All other photographs are from:
digitalSTOCK, digitalvision, ImageState, John Foxx, PhotoAlto, PhotoDisc, PhotoEssentials, PhotoPro, Stockbyte

All artworks are from the Miles Kelly Artwork Bank

Every effort has been made to acknowledge the source and copyright holder of each picture.
Miles Kelly Publishing apologizes for any unintentional errors or omissions.

Made with paper from a sustainable forest

www.mileskelly.net

Contents

Water world 6

Ocean features 8

Tides and shores 10

Life in a rock pool 12

Colourful coral 14

Swimming machines 16

Shark! 18

Whales and dolphins 20

Sleek swimmers 22

Ocean reptiles 24

Icy depths 26

Amazing journeys 28

On the wing 30

Perfect penguins 32

Harvests from the sea 34

First voyages 36

Pirates! 38

Going under 40

Superboats 42

Riding the waves 44

Ocean stories 46

Index 48

Water world

1 **Oceans cover more than two-thirds of the Earth's rocky surface.** Their total area is about 362 million square kilometres, which means there is more than twice as much ocean as land! Although all the oceans flow into each other, we know them as five different oceans – the Pacific, Atlantic, Indian, Southern and Arctic. Our landmasses, the continents, rise out of the oceans.

ATLANTIC OCEAN

PACIFIC OCEAN

2 **The largest, deepest ocean is the Pacific.** It covers nearly half of our planet and is double the size of the Atlantic, the next largest ocean. In places, the Pacific is so deep that the Earth's tallest mountain, Everest, would sink without a trace.

▼ The point where the ocean meets the land is called the seashore.

3 **Oceans can look blue, green or grey.** This is because of the way light hits the surface. Water soaks up the red parts of light but scatters the blue-green parts, making the sea look different shades of blue or green.

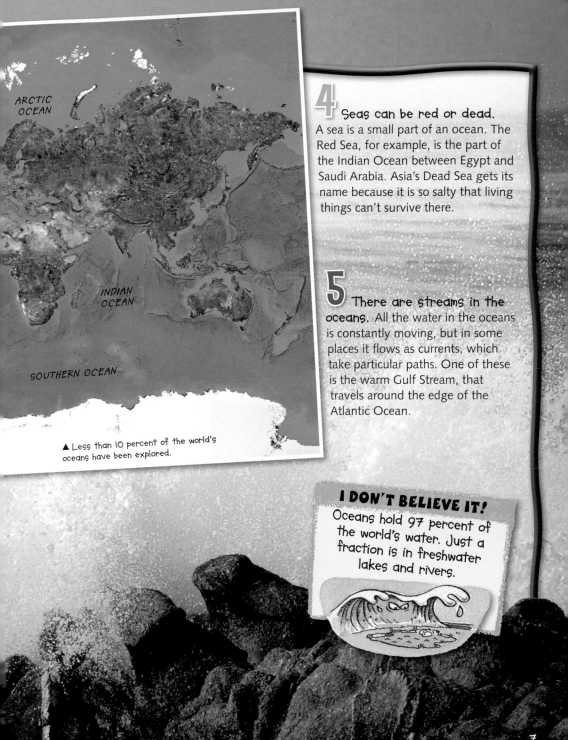

ARCTIC
OCEAN

INDIAN
OCEAN

SOUTHERN OCEAN

▲ Less than 10 percent of the world's
oceans have been explored.

4 Seas can be red or dead.
A sea is a small part of an ocean. The
Red Sea, for example, is the part of
the Indian Ocean between Egypt and
Saudi Arabia. Asia's Dead Sea gets its
name because it is so salty that living
things can't survive there.

5 There are streams in the
oceans. All the water in the oceans
is constantly moving, but in some
places it flows as currents, which
take particular paths. One of these
is the warm Gulf Stream, that
travels around the edge of the
Atlantic Ocean.

I DON'T BELIEVE IT!
Oceans hold 97 percent of
the world's water. Just a
fraction is in freshwater
lakes and rivers.

Ocean features

6 There are plains, mountains and valleys under the oceans, in areas called basins. Each basin has a rim (the flat continental shelf that meets the shore) and sides (the continental slope that drops away from the shelf). In the ocean basin there are flat abyssal plains, steep hills, huge underwater volcanoes called seamounts, and deep valleys called trenches.

Continental slope

Land

Continental shelf

Spreading ridge

Abyssal trench

Abyssal hills

▲ Under the oceans there is a landscape similar to that found on land.

▼ As the magma (molten rock) cools, the ocean floor spreads out.

Spreading floor

Ridge

Magma

7 The ocean floor is spreading. Molten (liquid) rock inside the Earth seeps from holes on the seabed. As the rock cools, it forms new sections of floor that creep slowly out. Scientists have proved this fact by looking at layers of rock on the ocean floor. There are matching stripes of rock either side of a ridge. Each pair came from the same hot rock eruption, then slowly spread out.

Seamount

Volcanic island

Ocean trench

8 Some islands are swallowed by the ocean. Sometimes, a ring-shaped coral reef called an atoll marks where a volcanic island once was. The coral reef built up around the island. After the volcano sank underwater, the reef remained.

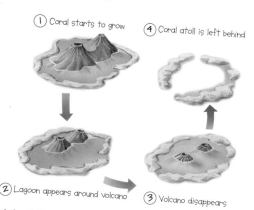

① Coral starts to grow

④ Coral atoll is left behind

② Lagoon appears around volcano

③ Volcano disappears

▲ An atoll is a ring-shaped coral reef that encloses a deep lagoon. It is left when an island sinks underwater.

9 New islands are born all the time. When an underwater volcano erupts, its lava cools in the water. Layers of lava build up, and the volcano grows in size. Eventually, it is tall enough to peep above the waves. The Hawaiian islands rose from the sea like this.

I DON'T BELIEVE IT!
The world's longest mountain chain is under the ocean. It is the Mid-Ocean range and stretches around the middle of the Earth.

▶ The Hawaiian islands were built up from layers of lava. There are still more to come.

Tides and shores

10 **The sea level rises and falls twice each day along the coast.** This is known as high and low tides. Tides happen because of the pull of the Moon's gravity, which lifts water from the part of Earth's surface facing it.

▼ At high tide, the sea rises up the shore and dumps seaweed, shells and driftwood. Most coasts have two high tides and two low tides every day.

High tides happen at the same time each day on opposite sides of the Earth

At high tide the water level rises

At low tide the water level goes down again

11 **Spring tides are especially high.** They occur twice a month, when the Moon is in line with the Earth and the Sun. Then, the Sun's pulling force joins the Moon's and seawater is lifted higher than usual. The opposite happens when the Moon and Sun are at right angles to each other. Then, their pulling powers work against each other causing weak neap tides – the lowest high tides and low tides.

► Spring tides occur when the Sun and the Moon are lined up and pulling together.

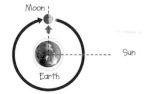

◄ Neap tides occur when the Sun and Moon are at right angles to each other and pulling in different directions.

12
The sea is strong enough to carve into rock. Pounding waves batter coastlines and erode, or wear away, the rock.

▼ Erosion can create amazing shapes such as arches, and pillars called sea stacks.

Sea stack

Arch

I DON'T BELIEVE IT!

The biggest tsunami was taller than five Statues of Liberty! It hit the Japanese Ryuku Islands in 1771.

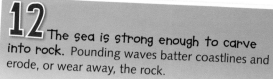

13
Tsunamis are the most powerful waves. They happen when underwater earthquakes trigger tremendous shock waves. These whip up a wall of water that travels across the ocean's surface.

14
Sand is found on bars and spits, as well as beaches. It is made up of grains of worn-down rock and shell. Sand collects on shorelines and spits, but also forms on offshore beaches called sand bars. Spits are narrow ridges of worn sand and pebbles.

15
Some shores are swampy. This makes the border between land and sea hard to pinpoint. Muddy coastlines include tropical mangrove swamps that are flooded by salty water from the sea.

▶ The stilt roots of mangrove trees can take in nutrients from the water.

Life in a rock pool

16 **Rock pools are teeming with all kinds of creatures.** Limpets are a kind of shellfish. They live on rocks and in pools at shorelines. Here, they eat slimy, green algae, but they have to withstand the crashing tide. They cling to the rock with their muscular foot, only moving when the tide is out.

Quiz

Can you find the names of four shells in the puzzle below?
1. alcm 2. lesmus
3. teroys 4. hewkl

Answers:
1. Clam 2. Mussel
3. Oyster 4. Whelk

17 **Some anemones fight with harpoons.** Beadlet anemones will sometimes fight over a feeding ground. Their weapon is the poison they usually use to stun their prey. They shoot tiny hooks like harpoons at each other until the weakest one gives in.

▶ Anemones are named after flowers, because of their petal-like arms.

▶ Starfish are relatives of brittle stars, sea urchins and sea cucumbers.

18 **Starfish can grow new arms.** They may have as many as 40 arms, or rays. If a predator grabs hold of one, the starfish abandons the ray, and uses the others to make its getaway!

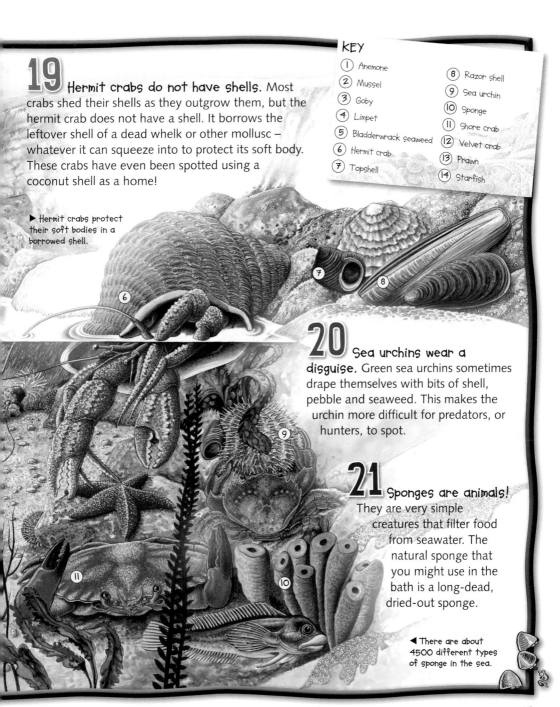

19 **Hermit crabs do not have shells.** Most crabs shed their shells as they outgrow them, but the hermit crab does not have a shell. It borrows the leftover shell of a dead whelk or other mollusc – whatever it can squeeze into to protect its soft body. These crabs have even been spotted using a coconut shell as a home!

▶ Hermit crabs protect their soft bodies in a borrowed shell.

KEY

1. Anemone
2. Mussel
3. Goby
4. Limpet
5. Bladderwrack seaweed
6. Hermit crab
7. Topshell
8. Razor shell
9. Sea urchin
10. Sponge
11. Shore crab
12. Velvet crab
13. Prawn
14. Starfish

20 **Sea urchins wear a disguise.** Green sea urchins sometimes drape themselves with bits of shell, pebble and seaweed. This makes the urchin more difficult for predators, or hunters, to spot.

21 **Sponges are animals!** They are very simple creatures that filter food from seawater. The natural sponge that you might use in the bath is a long-dead, dried-out sponge.

◀ There are about 4500 different types of sponge in the sea.

Colourful coral

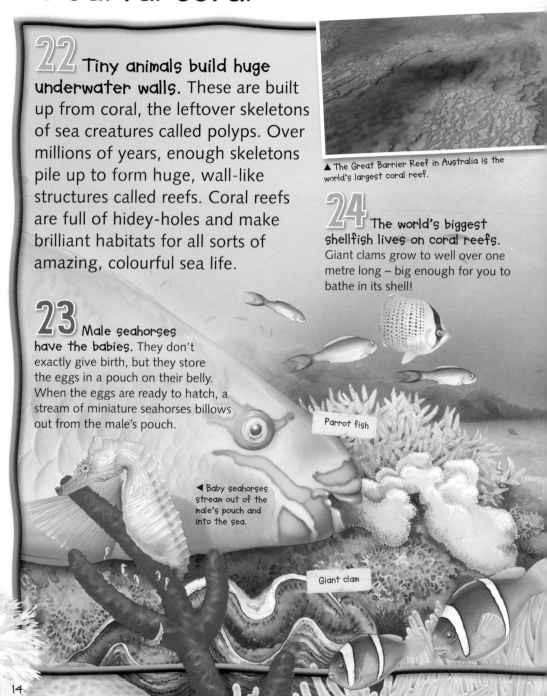

22 **Tiny animals build huge underwater walls.** These are built up from coral, the leftover skeletons of sea creatures called polyps. Over millions of years, enough skeletons pile up to form huge, wall-like structures called reefs. Coral reefs are full of hidey-holes and make brilliant habitats for all sorts of amazing, colourful sea life.

▲ The Great Barrier Reef in Australia is the world's largest coral reef.

24 **The world's biggest shellfish lives on coral reefs.** Giant clams grow to well over one metre long – big enough for you to bathe in its shell!

23 **Male seahorses have the babies.** They don't exactly give birth, but they store the eggs in a pouch on their belly. When the eggs are ready to hatch, a stream of miniature seahorses billows out from the male's pouch.

Parrot fish

◄ Baby seahorses stream out of the male's pouch and into the sea.

Giant clam

25 Some fish go to the cleaners. Cleaner wrasse are little fish that are paid for cleaning! Larger fish, such as groupers and moray eels visit the wrasse, which eat all the parasites and other bits of dirt off the bigger fishes' bodies – what a feast!

26 Clownfish are sting-proof. Most creatures steer clear of an anemone's stinging tentacles. But the clownfish swims among the stingers, where it's safe from predators. Strangely, the anemone doesn't seem to sting the clownfish.

27 Some fish look like stones. Stone fish rest on the seabed, looking just like the rocks that surround them. If they are spotted, the poisonous spines on their backs can stun an attacker in seconds.

I DON'T BELIEVE IT!
You can see the Great Barrier Reef from space! At over 2000 kilometres long, it is the largest structure ever built by living creatures.

Lion fish

Cleaner wrasse fish

Stone fish

Clownfish

▲ Tropical coral reefs are the habitat of an amazing range of marine plants and creatures.

Swimming machines

28 **There are over 21,000 different types of fish in the sea.** They range from huge whale sharks to tiny gobies. Almost all are covered in scales and use fins and a muscular tail to power through the water. Like their freshwater cousins, sea fish have slits called gills that take oxygen from the water so they can breathe.

▶ In a large group called a school, fish like these yellow snappers have less chance of being picked off by a predator.

29 **The oarfish is bigger than an oar – it can be as long as four canoes!** It is the longest bony fish and is found in all the world's oceans. Oarfish are striking creatures – they have a red fin along the length of their back.

◀ People once thought oarfish swam horizontally through the water. Now they know they swim upright.

30 **Sunfish like sunbathing!** Ocean sunfish are very large, broad fish that can weigh up to one tonne. They are named after their habit of sunbathing on the surface of the ocean.

◀ At over 3 metres long, sunfish are the biggest bony fish in the oceans. They feed on plankton.

31 **Flying fish cannot really fly.** Fish can't survive out of water, but flying fish sometimes leap above the waves when they are travelling at high speeds. They use their wing-like fins to keep them in the air for as long as 30 seconds.

▲ Flying fish feed near the surface so they are easy to find. Their gliding flight helps them escape most hunters.

QUIZ

1. Which fish like to sunbathe?
2. How many types of fish live in the sea?
3. How does a fish breathe?
4. Can flying fish really fly?

Answers:
1. Sunfish 2. Over 21,000 3. With its gills 4. No

32 Not all fish are the same shape. Cod or mackerel are what we think of as a normal fish shape, but fish come in all shapes and sizes. Flounder and other flatfish have squashed-flat bodies. Eels are so long and thin that the biggest types look like snakes, while tiny garden eels resemble worms! And of course, seahorses and seadragons look nothing like other fish at all!

▶ The flounder's flattened shape and dull colouring help to camouflage (hide) it on the seabed.

Shark!

▼ Great white sharks are fierce hunters. They will attack and eat almost anything, but prefer to feed on seals.

33 **Great whites are the scariest sharks in the oceans.** These powerful predators have been known to kill people and can speed through the water at 30 kilometres an hour. Unlike most fish, the great white is warm-blooded. This allows its muscles to work well, but also means the shark has to feed on plenty of meat.

▶ Basking sharks eat enormous amounts of plankton, which they sieve from the water as they swim.

34 Most sharks are meat-eaters. Herring are a favourite food for sand tiger and thresher sharks, while a tiger shark will eat just about anything! Strangely, some of the biggest sharks take the smallest prey. Whale sharks and basking sharks eat tiny sea creatures called plankton.

35

Sharks are shaped like torpedos. Most sharks are built for speed, with a long streamlined body. This means water can move past them easily. A shark's fins keep it the right way up in the water, and help it to change direction quickly, so it can chase its prey. Sharks also have special cells in their heads, called ampullae of Lorenzini. These allow them to sense electricity given out by nearby fish.

I DON'T BELIEVE IT!

Some sharks, such as dogfish and zebra sharks, don't look after their pups. They leave them to fend for themselves.

Nostril

Dorsal fin

Jaw

Ampullae of Lorenzini

▶ The different features of a shark's body help it to be a successful hunter.

Gill

Pectoral fin

Pelvic fin

Anal fin

Tail fin

36

Hammerhead sharks have a hammer-shaped head! With a nostril and an eye on each end of the 'hammer', they swing their head from side to side. This gives them double the chance to see and sniff out any signs of a tasty catch.

▲ Hammerheads prey on other sharks and rays, bony fish, crabs and lobsters, octopus and squid.

19

Whales and dolphins

37 **The biggest animal on the planet lives in the oceans.** It is the blue whale, measuring about 28 metres in length and weighing up to 190 tonnes. It feeds by filtering tiny, shrimp-like creatures called krill from the water – about four tonnes of krill a day! Like other great whales, it has special, sieve-like parts in its mouth called baleen plates.

▶ The blue whale can be found in every ocean except the Arctic.

38 **Killer whales play with their food.** They especially like to catch baby seals, which they toss into the air before eating. Killer whales are not true whales, but the largest dolphins. They have teeth for chewing, instead of baleen plates.

▼ As the sperm whale surfaces, it pushes out stale air through its blowhole. It fills its lungs with fresh air and dives down again.

39 **Whales and dolphins have to come to the surface for air.** This is because they are mammals, like we are. Sperm whales hold their breath the longest. They have been known to stay underwater for nearly two hours.

40 Dolphins and whales sing songs to communicate. The noisiest is the humpback whale, whose wailing noises can be heard for hundreds of kilometres. The sweetest is the beluga – nicknamed the 'sea canary'. Songs are used to attract a mate, or just to keep track of each other.

▲ The beluga is a type of white whale. It makes a range of noises – whistles, clangs, chirps and moos!

42 Moby-Dick was a famous white whale. It featured in *Moby-Dick* (1851), a book by Herman Melville about a white sperm whale and a whaler called Captain Ahab.

41 The narwhal has a horn like a unicorn's. This Arctic whale has a long, twirly tooth that spirals out of its head. The males use their tusks as a weapon when they are fighting over females.

▲ A male narwhal's tusk can grow to over 2 metres long.

I DON'T BELIEVE IT!
Barnacles are shellfish. They attach themselves to ships' hulls, or the bodies of grey whales and other large sea animals.

Sleek swimmers

43 **Whales and dolphins are not the only sea mammals.** Seals, sea lions and walruses are warm-blooded mammals that have adapted to ocean life. These creatures are known as pinnipeds, meaning they have flippers instead of legs. They also have streamlined bodies and a layer of fatty blubber under the skin, to keep them warm in chilly waters.

▼ Most seals live in cold waters. These crabeater seals live in Antarctica, as do leopard, Weddell, and fur seals. Northern seals, which live around the Arctic, include harp and bearded seals.

▼ Fights between male elephant seals during the breeding season can be extremely violent.

44 **Elephant seals are well-named — they are truly enormous!** Southern elephant seal males can weigh over 3.5 tonnes, while their northern cousins weigh at least 2 tonnes. During their three-month-long breeding season, males stay ashore to fight off rivals. Unable to hunt for fish, some lose as much as half their body weight.

45 **Walruses seem to change colour!** When a walrus is in the water, it appears pale brown or even white. This is because blood drains from the skin's surface to stop the body losing heat. On land, the blood returns to the skin and walruses can look reddish brown or pink.

▼ Walruses use their tusks as weapons. They are also used to make breathing holes in the ice, and to help the walrus pull itself out of the water.

I DON'T BELIEVE IT!

Leopard seals sing in their sleep! These seals, found in the Antarctic, chirp and whistle while they snooze.

▼ Anchored to the kelp, a sea otter is free to rest.

46 **Sea otters anchor themselves when they sleep.** These playful creatures live off the Pacific coast among huge forests of giant seaweed called kelp. When they sleep, they wrap a strand of kelp around their body to stop them being washed out to sea.

Ocean reptiles

47 **Marine iguanas are the most seaworthy lizards.** Most lizards prefer life on land, where it is easier to warm up their cold-blooded bodies, but marine iguanas depend on the sea for food. They dive underwater to graze. When on land, the iguanas' dark skin absorbs the Sun's heat.

▼ Marine iguanas are found around the Galapagos Islands in the Pacific. They dive into the water to graze on seaweed and the algae growing on rocks.

▼ Female green turtles use their flippers to dig a large nest. Once they have laid their eggs, they cover the nest with sand.

48 **Turtles come ashore only to lay their eggs.** Although they are born on land, turtles head for the sea the minute they hatch. Females return to the beach where they were born to dig their nests. After they have laid their eggs, they go straight back to the water. Hawksbill turtles may lay up to 140 eggs in a clutch, while some green turtle females clock up 800 eggs in a year!

49 There are venomous (poisonous) snakes in the sea. Most stay close to land and come ashore to lay their eggs. Banded sea snakes, for example, cruise around coral reefs in search of their favourite food – eels. But the yellow-bellied sea snake never leaves the water. It gives birth to live babies in the open ocean.

▶ Banded sea snakes use venom (poison) to stun their prey.

▼ The yellow-bellied sea snake uses its colourful underside to attract fish. It then darts back – so the fish are next to its open mouth!

Banded sea snake

Yellow-bellied sea snake

50 Leatherback turtles dive up to 1200 metres for food. They hold the record for being the biggest sea turtles and for making the deepest dives. Leatherbacks feed mostly on jellyfish but their diet also includes molluscs, crabs, lobsters and starfish.

QUIZ
1. Where are marine iguanas found?
2. Why do turtles come ashore?
3. Where do banded sea snakes search for food?
4. How deep can leatherback turtles dive?

Answers:
1. Around the Galapagos Islands 2. To lay their eggs 3. Coral reefs 4. Up to 1200 metres

▼ Leatherbacks are the biggest turtles in the world and can grow to 2 metres in length.

Icy depths

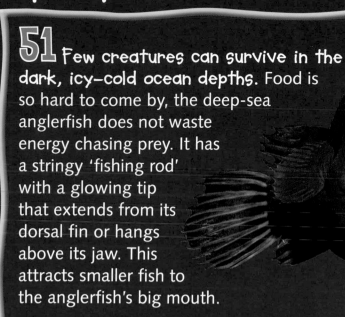

51 Few creatures can survive in the dark, icy-cold ocean depths. Food is so hard to come by, the deep-sea anglerfish does not waste energy chasing prey. It has a stringy 'fishing rod' with a glowing tip that extends from its dorsal fin or hangs above its jaw. This attracts smaller fish to the anglerfish's big mouth.

▲ Anglerfish are black or brown for camouflage. Only their glowing 'fishing rod' is visible in the gloom.

Lantern fish

Cookie-cutter shark

Hatchet fish

52 Some deep-sea fish glow in the dark. As well as tempting prey, light also confuses predators. About 1500 different deep-sea fish give off light. The lantern fish's whole body glows. The hatchet fish produces light along its belly and has silvery scales on its sides, which reflect light, confusing predators. Just the belly of the cookie-cutter shark gives off a ghostly glow.

◀ The light created by deep-sea fish, or by bacteria living on their bodies, is known as biological light, or bioluminescence.

53 Black swallowers are greedy-guts! These strange fish are just 25 centimetres long but can eat fish far bigger than themselves. Their loose jaws unhinge to fit over the prey. Then the stretchy body expands to take in their enormous meal.

54 Viperfish have teeth that are invisible in the dark. They swim around with their jaws wide open. Deep-sea shrimp often see nothing until they are right inside the viperfish's mouth.

▶ The viperfish is named for its long, snake-like fangs.

55 On the seabed, there are worms as long as cars! These are giant tubeworms and they cluster around hot spots on the ocean floor. They feed on tiny particles that they filter from the water.

▲ The black swallower's stomach can stretch to take in prey twice its length.

▼ Bacteria inside the tubeworm turn minerals into food that the worm needs to survive.

Plume

Bacteria

Heart

Blood Vessel

Tube

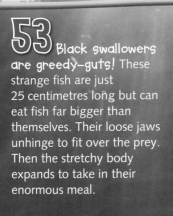

I DON'T BELIEVE IT!
Female deep-sea anglerfish grow to 120 centimetres in length, but the males are a tiny 6 centimetres!

Amazing journeys

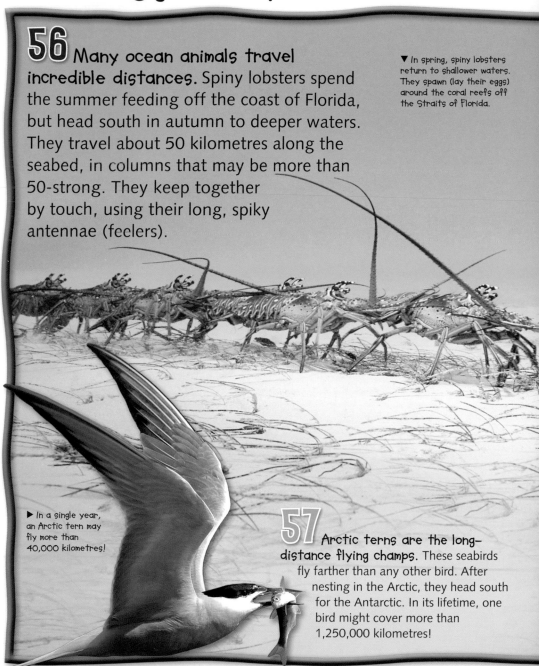

56 Many ocean animals travel incredible distances. Spiny lobsters spend the summer feeding off the coast of Florida, but head south in autumn to deeper waters. They travel about 50 kilometres along the seabed, in columns that may be more than 50-strong. They keep together by touch, using their long, spiky antennae (feelers).

▼ In spring, spiny lobsters return to shallower waters. They spawn (lay their eggs) around the coral reefs off the Straits of Florida.

▶ In a single year, an Arctic tern may fly more than 40,000 kilometres!

57 Arctic terns are the long-distance flying champs. These seabirds fly farther than any other bird. After nesting in the Arctic, they head south for the Antarctic. In its lifetime, one bird might cover more than 1,250,000 kilometres!

58 Grey whales migrate, or travel, farther than any other mammal. There are two main grey whale populations in the Pacific. One spends summer off the Alaskan coast. In winter they migrate south to Mexico to breed. The whales may swim nearly 20,000 kilometres in a year. The other grey whale group spends summer off the coast of Russia, then travels south to Korea.

1 Grey whales travel south to Mexico in winter to have their babies

2 In summer the whales swim back to the food-rich waters off the coast of Alaska

▲ Grey whales spend summer in the Bering Sea, feeding on tiny, shrimp-like creatures called amphipods. They spend their breeding season, December to March, in warmer waters.

I DON'T BELIEVE IT!
Eels and salmon swim thousands of kilometres from the sea to spawn in the same river nurseries where they were born.

▲ As soon as they are born, loggerhead hatchlings crawl down to the water, to avoid being picked off by hungry gulls or crabs.

59 Baby loggerhead turtles make a two-year journey. They are born on beaches in Japan. The hatchlings hurry down to the sea and set off across the Pacific to Mexico, a journey of 10,000 kilometres. They spend about five years there before returning to Japan to breed.

On the wing

QUIZ

1. How long is the wingspan of an albatross?
2. Where do puffins dig their burrows?
3. How do gannets dive for fish?
4. What colour is a male frigate bird's pouch?

Answers:
1. Around 3 metres 2. On clifftops
3. Headfirst into the ocean
4. Bright red

60 **Wandering albatrosses are the biggest seabirds.** An albatross has a wingspan of around 3 metres – about the length of a family car! These seabirds are so large, they take off by launching from a cliff. Albatrosses spend months at sea. To feed, they land on the sea, where they sit and catch creatures such as squid.

▶ Albatrosses are such expert gliders that they can even sleep on the wing.

▼ Puffins often scrape their own burrows on clifftops, or they may take over an abandoned rabbit hole.

61 **Puffins nest in burrows.** While many birds jostle for space on a high cliff edge, puffins dig a burrow on the clifftop. Here, they lay a single egg. Both parents feed the chick for the first 6 weeks.

62 **Gannets wear air-bag shock absorbers.** The gannet's feeding technique is to plummet headfirst into the ocean and catch a fish in its beak. It dives at high-speed and hits the water hard. Luckily, the gannet's head is protected with sacs of air that absorb most of the shock.

63 **Frigate birds puff up a balloon for their mate.** Male frigate birds have a bright-red pouch on their throat. They inflate, or blow up, the pouch as part of their display to attract a female.

▲ When a gannet spots its meal, it dives into the water at high speed to catch it.

▼ A frigate bird shows off to its mate.

▶ A blue-footed booby displays its blue feet.

64 **Boobies dance to attract a mate.** There are two types of booby, blue- or red-footed. The dancing draws attention to the male's colourful feet. Perhaps this stops the females from mating with the wrong type of bird.

Perfect penguins

65 **Macaroni, Chinstrap, Jackass and Emperor are all types of penguin.** There are 17 different types in total, and most live around the Antarctic. Penguins feed on fish, squid and krill. Their black-and-white plumage is important camouflage. Seen from above, a penguin's black back blends in with the water. The white belly is hard to distinguish from the sunlit surface of the sea.

66 **Penguins can swim, but not fly.** They have oily, waterproofed feathers and flipper-like wings. Instead of lightweight, hollow bones – like a flying bird's – some penguins have solid, heavy bones. This enables them to stay underwater longer when diving for food. Emperor penguins can stay under for 15 minutes or more.

67 **Some penguins build stone circles.** This is the way that Adélie and Gentoo penguins build nests on the shingled shores where they breed. First, they scrape out a small dip with their flippered feet and then they surround the hollow with a circle of pebbles.

▲ An Adélie penguin builds its nest from stones and small rocks.

▼ King penguins live near Antarctica. Like all penguins, they have a layer of fat under their feathers to protect them in the icy water.

▼ The different types of penguin vary in shape, size and appearance.

Rockhopper   Macaroni   Royal   Chinstrap   Gentoo

I DON'T BELIEVE IT!

The fastest swimming bird is the Gentoo penguin. It has been known to swim at speeds of 27 kilometres an hour!

68 **Emperor penguin dads balance an egg on their feet.** They do this to keep their egg off the Antarctic ice, where it would freeze. The female leaves her mate with the egg for the whole two months that it takes to hatch. The male has to go without food during this time. When the chick hatches, the mother returns and both parents help to raise it.

▶ A downy Emperor penguin chick cannot find its own food in the sea until it has grown its waterproof, adult plumage. In the meantime, its parents feed and care for it.

33

Harvests from the sea

69 Oysters come from beds – and lobsters from pots! The animals in the oceans feed other sea creatures, and they feed us, too! To gather oysters, fishermen raise them on trays or poles in the water. First, they collect oyster larvae, or babies. They attract them by putting out sticks hung with shells. Lobster larvae are too difficult to collect, but the adults are caught in pots filled with fish bait.

▲ Bait is placed in lobster pots like these. Once a lobster has entered, it can't escape.

70 Some farmers grow seaweed. Seaweed is delicious to eat, and is also a useful ingredient in products such as ice cream and plant fertilizer. In shallow, tropical waters, people grow their own on plots of seabed.

▼ A woman harvests seaweed on a farm on the coast of Zanzibar, East Africa.

71 **Sea minerals are big business.** Minerals are useful substances that we mine from the ground – and oceans are full of them! The most valuable are oil and gas, which are pumped from the seabed and piped ashore or transported in huge supertankers. Salt is another important mineral. In hot, low-lying areas, people build walls to hold shallow pools of sea water. The water dries up in the sun, leaving behind crystals of salt.

72 **There are gemstones under the sea.** Pearls are made by oysters. If a grain of sand is lodged inside an oyster's shell, it irritates its soft body. The oyster coats the sand with a substance called nacre, which is also used to line the inside of the shell. Over the years, more nacre builds up and the pearl gets bigger.

▲ The oil platform's welded–steel legs rest on the seabed. They support the platform around 15 metres above the surface of the water.

▶ An oyster's shell must be pried open with a knife to get to the pearl inside.

QUIZ

1. What are the young of lobster called?

2. What substances are pumped from the seabed?

3. Is seaweed edible?

4. Which gemstone is made by oysters?

Answers:
1. Larvae 2. Oil and gas
3. Yes 4. Pearl

First voyages

73 **The first boats were made from tree trunks.** Early people hollowed out tree trunks to craft their own dug-outs. For several hundred years, the Maori peoples of New Zealand made log war canoes, decorating them with beautiful carvings.

▼ Maori war canoes were usually carved out of kauri pine trunks.

74 **Greek warships were oar–some!** The ancient Greeks used people-power and sails to move their ships through the water. Triremes were warships rowed by three layers of oarsmen. In battle, the trireme was steered straight at an enemy ship like a battering ram.

▶ A painted eye on the trireme's hull was believed to protect the boat from evil spirits.

▼ Viking longboats were clinker-built, which means that they were made of overlapping planks of wood.

77 **Boats were used to find the way to a new world.** The 1400s were an amazing time of exploration and discovery. One explorer, Christopher Columbus, set sail from Spain in 1492 with a fleet of three ships. He hoped to find a new trade route to India, but instead he found the Americas. Before then, they were not even on the map!

75 **Dragons guarded Viking longboats.** Scandinavian seafarers decorated their boats' prows with carvings of dragons and serpents to terrify their enemies. Built from overlapping planks, Viking longboats were very seaworthy. Leif Ericson was the first Viking to cross the Atlantic Ocean to Newfoundland, in North America, just over 1000 years ago.

▼ Columbus's fleet consisted of the *Niña*, the *Pinta* and the *Santa Maria*.

76 **It is thought that Chinese navigators made the first compass–like device about 2500 years ago.** Compasses use the Earth's magnetism to show the directions of north, south, east and west. They are used at sea, where there are no landmarks. The navigators used lodestone, a naturally magnetic rock, to magnetize the needle.

▶ Early compasses were very simple. During the 1300s compasses became more detailed.

QUIZ

Unscramble the letters to find the names of six different types of boat.
1. leacvar 2. chenroos
3. rarlewt 4. coclear
5. leglay 6. pecpril

Answers:
1. Caravel 2. Schooner
3. Trawler 4. Coracle
5. Galley 6. Clipper

Pirates!

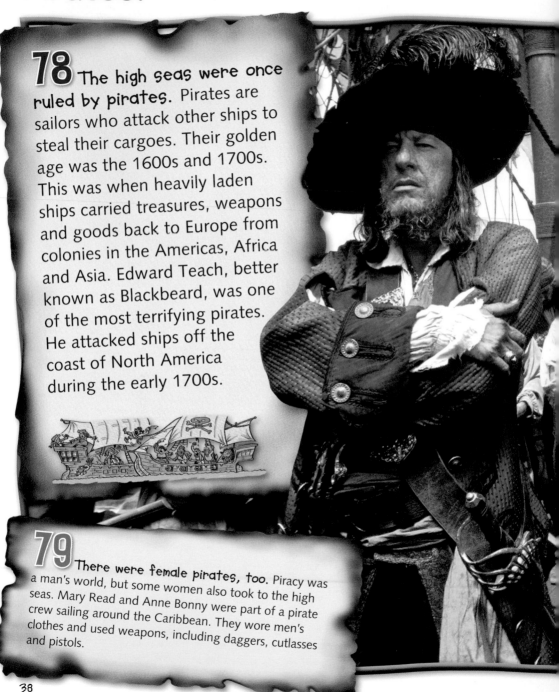

78 The high seas were once ruled by pirates. Pirates are sailors who attack other ships to steal their cargoes. Their golden age was the 1600s and 1700s. This was when heavily laden ships carried treasures, weapons and goods back to Europe from colonies in the Americas, Africa and Asia. Edward Teach, better known as Blackbeard, was one of the most terrifying pirates. He attacked ships off the coast of North America during the early 1700s.

79 There were female pirates, too. Piracy was a man's world, but some women also took to the high seas. Mary Read and Anne Bonny were part of a pirate crew sailing around the Caribbean. They wore men's clothes and used weapons, including daggers, cutlasses and pistols.

80
There are still pirates on the oceans. Despite police patrols that watch for pirates and smugglers, a few pirates still operate. Luxury yachts are an easy target and in the South China Sea, pirate gangs on motor boats even attack large merchant ships.

▶ Divers have found some extraordinary hoards of treasure on board sunken galleons.

▼ *Pirates of the Caribbean: The Curse of the Black Pearl* (2003) told the story of a group of pirates cursed for stealing treasure.

81
There is treasure lying under the sea. Over the centuries, many ships have sunk in storms or hit reefs. They include pirate ships loaded with stolen booty. Some ships were deliberately sunk by pirates. The bed of the Caribbean Sea is littered with the remains of Spanish galleons, many of which still hold treasure!

MAKE A PIRATE FLAG!

You will need:
paper paints brushes

The skull-and-crossbones is the most famous pirate flag, but it was not the only one. Copy one of these designs!

39

Going under

82 **A submarine has dived deeper than 10,000 metres.** The two-person *Trieste* made history in 1960 in an expedition to the Mariana Trench in the Pacific, the deepest part of any ocean. It took the submarine five hours to reach the bottom, a distance of 10,911 metres. On the way down, the extreme water pressure cracked part of the craft, but luckily, the two men inside returned to the surface unharmed.

▲ *Trieste* spent 20 minutes at the bottom of the Mariana Trench.

Mast to renew and expel air

Mine

◀ The Americans used *Turtle* against the British in their War of Independence.

Propellers

83 **The first combat submarine was shaped like an egg!** *Turtle* was a one-person submarine that made its test dive in 1776. It was the first real submarine. It did not have an engine – it was driven by a propeller turned by hand. *Turtle* was built for war. It travelled just below the surface and could fix bombs to the bottom of enemy ships.

84
Divers have a spare pair of lungs. Scuba divers wear special breathing apparatus called 'aqua lungs'. French divers, Jacques Cousteau and Emile Gagnan, came up with the idea of a portable oxygen supply. This meant that divers were able to swim freely for the first time, rather than wearing a heavy suit and helmet.

▲ Divers control their breathing to make their oxygen supply last as long as possible.

85
The biggest submarines weighed 26,500 tonnes. They were Russian submarines called Typhoons, built in the 1970s and 1980s. As well as being the biggest submarines, they were also the fastest, able to top 40 knots.

▼ The Typhoons did not need to come up to refuel because they were nuclear-powered.

Periscope

Rudder

Engine room

Living quarters

Torpedo firing tube

Diving plane

I DON'T BELIEVE IT!
In 1963 Jacques Cousteau built a village on the bed of the Red Sea. Along with four other divers, he lived there for a whole month.

Superboats

86 Some ships are invisible.

Stealth warships are not really invisible, of course, but they are hard to detect using radar. There are already materials being used for ships that can absorb some radar signals. Some paints can soak up radar, too, and signals are also bounced off in confusing directions by the ships' strange, angled hulls.

I DON'T BELIEVE IT!

People said *Titanic* was unsinkable. But in 1912 it hit an iceberg and sank on its maiden voyage. More than 1500 people drowned.

▶ An angled, sloping hull gives very little radar echo. This makes the stealth ship's location hard to pinpoint.

87 The biggest ship ever built was nearly half a kilometre long.

It was a supertanker called *Jahre Viking*. Supertankers carry cargoes of oil around the world. They move slowly because they are so huge and heavy. *Jahre Viking* was demolished in 2009. The world's biggest ship is now a container ship called *CMA CGM Marco Polo*.

▼ The giant supertanker *Jahre Viking* was just over 458 metres long.

▼ Hovercraft can travel at up to 65 knots, the equivalent of 120 kilometres an hour.

88 Not all boats ride the waves.

Hovercrafts sit slightly above the water. They have a rubbery 'skirt' that traps a cushion of air for them to ride on. Without the drag of the water to work against, hovercraft can cross the water much faster.

▼ On an aircraft carrier, planes are constantly taking off and landing, making the flight deck a very dangerous place.

89 Ships can give piggy-backs!

Heavy-lift ships can sink part of their deck underwater, so a smaller ship can sail aboard for a free ride. Some ships carry planes. Aircraft carriers transport planes that are too small to carry enough fuel for long distances. The deck doubles up as a runway, where the planes take off and land.

▼ Some cruise ships stop at different ports during the journey, while others only stop at the beginning and end.

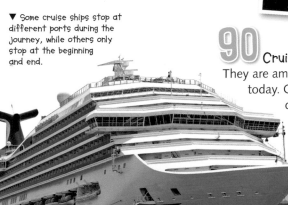

90 Cruise ships are floating holidays.

They are among the largest ships on the oceans today. Cruise ships usually have lots of different features, such as restaurants, shops, swimming pools, casinos, spas and bowling alleys. The biggest cruise ship in the world is currently *Allure of the Seas*, at over 360 metres in length.

Riding the waves

91 **The first sea sport was surfing.** It took off in the 1950s, but was invented centuries earlier in Hawaii, USA. Hawaii is still one of the best places to surf – at Waimea Bay, surfers catch waves that are up to 11 metres high. The record for the longest rides, though, are made off the coast of Mexico, where it is possible to surf for more than 1.5 kilometres.

▼ Modern surfboards are made of super-light materials. This means they create little drag in the water – and the surfer can reach high speeds!

92 **A single boat towed 100 water-skiers!** This record was made off the coast of Australia in 1986 and no one has beaten it yet. The drag boat was a cruiser called *Reef Cat.*

► Water-skiing is now one of the most popular of all water sports.

QUIZ

1. What was the name of the fastest hydroplane?
2. When did jet skis go on sale?
3. Where is Waimea Bay?
4. What is a trimaran?

Answers:
1. Spirit of Australia
2. 1973 3. Hawaii
4. A three-hulled boat

44

▼ Jet skis first went on sale in 1973.

94 **Three hulls are sometimes better than one.** Powerboating is an exciting, dangerous sport. Competitors are always trying out new boat designs that will race even faster. Multi-hulled boats minimize drag, but keep the boat steady. Trimarans have three slender, streamlined hulls that cut through the water.

93 **Jet-skiers can travel at nearly 100 kilometres an hour.** Jet skis were first developed in the 1960s. Their inventor was an American called Clayton Jacobsen who wanted to combine his two favourite hobbies, motorbikes and water-skiing. Today, some jet-skiers are professional sportspeople.

► Trimarans have three hulls, while catamarans have two.

95 **Hydroplanes fly over the waves.** They are a cross between a boat and a plane. Special 'wings' raise the hull 2 metres above the water. The fastest hydroplane ever was *Spirit of Australia*. Driven by Kenneth Warby, it sped along at more than 500 kilometres an hour above the surface of the water!

▲ Hydroplanes are motor boats that skim across the surface of the water.

Ocean stories

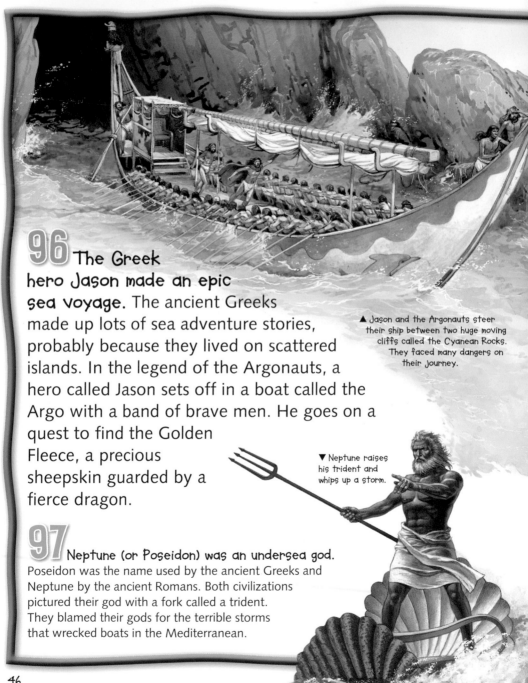

96 The Greek hero Jason made an epic sea voyage. The ancient Greeks made up lots of sea adventure stories, probably because they lived on scattered islands. In the legend of the Argonauts, a hero called Jason sets off in a boat called the Argo with a band of brave men. He goes on a quest to find the Golden Fleece, a precious sheepskin guarded by a fierce dragon.

▲ Jason and the Argonauts steer their ship between two huge moving cliffs called the Cyanean Rocks. They faced many dangers on their journey.

▼ Neptune raises his trident and whips up a storm.

97 Neptune (or Poseidon) was an undersea god. Poseidon was the name used by the ancient Greeks and Neptune by the ancient Romans. Both civilizations pictured their god with a fork called a trident. They blamed their gods for the terrible storms that wrecked boats in the Mediterranean.

The beautiful goddess Aphrodite emerges from the sea.

99
Long ago, people believed in a giant sea monster, called the **kraken.** The stories were used to explain the dangers of the sea. Sightings of the giant squid might have inspired these tales.

▶ Mistaken for a monster! The 15-metre-long giant squid has eyes as big as dinner plates.

98
The Greek goddess of love was born in the sea. Aphrodite was said to be the daughter of Zeus, the king of the gods. She was born out of the foam of the sea. The Romans based their love goddess, Venus, on the same story. Lots of artists have painted her rising from the waves in a giant clam shell.

100
Mermaids lured sailors to their deaths on the rocks. Mythical mermaids were said to be half-woman, half-fish. Folklore tells how the mermaids confused sailors with their beautiful singing – with the result that their ships were wrecked on the rocks.

▼ Mermaids were said to have the tail of a fish instead of legs.

I DON'T BELIEVE IT!
A mermaid's purse is the name given to the eggcases of the dog shark. They look a little bit like handbags!

Index

Entries in **bold** refer to main subject entries. Entries in *italics* refer to illustrations.

A
abyssal plains 8
Adélie penguins 32, *32*
aircraft carriers 43, *43*
albatrosses **30**, *30*
algae 12, *24*
anglerfish **26**, *26, 27*
Antarctic 32
Aphrodite (goddess) **47**, *47*
Arctic Ocean 6
Arctic terns **28**, *28*
Argo 46
Atlantic Ocean 6, 7
atolls 9, *9*

B
bacteria *26, 27*
baleen plates 20
basking sharks 18, *18*
beluga whales 21, *21*
bioluminescence 26
black swallowers **27**, *27*
blue whales **20**, *20*
boats **36**, *37*
boobies **31**, *31*

C
camouflage *17, 26,* 32
canoes 36, *36*
clownfish **15**, *15*
Columbus, Christopher 37, *37*
compasses **37**, *37*
continental shelf 8, *8*
continental slope 8, *8*
coral reefs 9, **14**, *15,* 25
Cousteau, Jacques 41
cruise ships **43**, *43*
currents 7

D
Dead Sea 7
deep-sea fish **26–27**
dolphins 20, 21, 22

E
earthquakes, underwater 11
eels 29
elephant seals **22**, *22*
Emperor penguins 32, 33, *33*
erosion **11**, *11*

F
feathers, penguin 32
fins 16, 19, *19*
fish **15**, **16–17**, *16, 17*
  deep-sea **26–27**

G
gannets **31**, *31*
gas 35
giant clams **14**, *14*
giant squid 47, *47*
gills 16, *19*
Great Barrier Reef *14,* 15
great white sharks **18**, *18*
green turtles 24, *24*
grey whales **29**, *29*

H, I
hammerhead sharks **19**, *19*
hawksbill turtles 24
hermit crabs **13**, *13*
hovercraft **43**, *43*
humpback whales 21
hydroplanes **45**, *45*
Indian Ocean 6, 7
islands **9**, *9*

K
killer whales **20**
king penguins 32

L
leatherback turtles **25**, *25*
limpets **12**, *12*
lobsters 28, *28,* 34, *34*
loggerhead turtles 29, *29*

M, N
mammals 20, 22
mangrove swamps 11, *11*
marine iguanas **24**, *24*

mermaids 47, *47*
migrations **28–29**, *29*
minerals **35**
mining, undersea 35
mountains, undersea 9
narwhals **21**, *21*
neap tides **10**, *10*
Neptune (god) 46, *46*

O
oarfish **16**, *16*
ocean floor spreading 8, *8*
oceans **6–7**
oil 35, *35,* 42
oysters 34, 35, *35*

P, R
Pacific Ocean **6**, 29
pearls 35, *35*
penguins **32–33**, *32, 33*
pinnipeds 22
pirates **38–39**, *38–39*
Poseidon (god) 46
puffins **30**, *30*
reptiles, ocean **24–25**
rock pools **12–13**

S
sails 36
salmon 29
salt 35
sand **11**
scuba divers **41**, *41*
sea anemones 12, *12,* 15
sea lions 22
sea otters **23**, *23*
sea snakes **25**, *25*
sea urchins **13**, *13*
seabed 8
seabirds **30–31**
seahorses **14**, *14, 17*
seals 22, *22,* 23
seamounts 8, *9*
seas **7**
seaweed 13, **34**, *34*
sharks **18–19**, *18, 19,* 26, 47
shellfish 12, 14, *14*
ships 38, *38,* 39, *39,* 42, *42,* 43, *43,* 46, *46*

shores 11
snakes, sea **25**, *25*
Southern Ocean 6
sperm whales 20, *20*
sponges **13**, *13*
sports, water **44–45**
spring tides **10**, *10*
starfish **12**, *12*
stealth ships **42**, *42*
stone fish 15, *15*
submarines **40–41**, *40, 41*
sunfish **16**, *16*
supertankers 35, **42**, *42*
surfing **44**, *44*

T
tides **10**, *10*
Titanic 42
trenches 8, *9*
Trieste 40, *40*
trimarans 45, *45*
triremes 36, *36*
tsunamis **11**
tubeworms **27**, *27*
turtles **24**, *24,* 25, *25,* 29, *29*

V
Venus (goddess) **47**
Viking longboats 37, *37*
viperfish **27**, *27*
volcanoes, undersea 8, 9, *9*

W
walruses 22, **23**, *23*
wandering albatrosses 30
warships **36**, *36*
water-skiing **44**, *44*
water sports **44–45**
whale sharks 18
whales **20–21**, 22, 29